STRATEGIES
FOR
READING NONFICTION
COMPREHENSION & STUDY ACTIVITIES

GRADES 4 - 8

Sandra M. Simons, Ph.D.

SPRING·STREET·PRESS

Eugene, Oregon

ISBN 0-9627689-1-X

Cover design: Jean McCandless, Los Altos Hills, California
                       Judy Sanfilippo, Eugene, Oregon

Page design: Gene Floersch, Beach Studios, Inc., Melbourne Beach, Florida

CONTENTS

TO THE TEACHER

Strategies for Reading Nonfiction: Comprehension and Study Activities is an extremely valuable teaching aid designed for use in reading classrooms and in subject area classes across the curriculum. It contains over 40 reproducible *Comprehension and Study Activity* masters that may be used with any nonfiction selection – trade books, textbooks, and periodicals. It also contains 10 *Strategy Guides* to help students learn and apply essential reading and study strategies. The *Comprehension and Study Activities* and the *Strategy Guides* may be used in a variety of ways to adapt to your reading or subject area curriculum and your teaching style. Additionally, the *Comprehension and Study Activities* accommodate the needs of a variety of abilities and different learning styles within your regular classroom instruction.

Goals

The primary goals of **Strategies for Reading Nonfiction** are
- to help students become independent, strategic readers and learners
- to improve students' ability to construct meaning from nonfiction text
- to help students become competent using a variety of active reading and studying strategies
- to develop a positive attitude about oneself as a reader and learner

Components

COMPREHENSION AND STUDY ACTIVITIES

Before and After Reading Activities

<u>The General Activities</u> have two parts: a prereading activity which prepares students for reading and a follow-up postreading activity which helps students integrate new learning and reflect on their reading. The activities may be used alone or in conjunction with each other.
- **Before Reading Activities** promote active reading by helping students access prior knowledge, focus attention, and set purposes for reading.
- **The Postreading Activities** require students to select main ideas, organize information, summarize new learning, and evaluate their own comprehension.

Components

The Vocabulary Activities promote independent word learning. They may be used before reading to introduce students to unfamiliar words they will encounter in the text or after reading to solidify their understanding of new words.

While You Read Activities

While You Read Activities develop comprehension monitoring strategies. The activities guide students to check their understanding during reading by having them periodically stop to self-question, predict, reset purposes, and summarize main ideas and direct them to use fix-up strategies when comprehension fails. **While You Read Activities** help students understand how to think as they read.

After Reading Activities

General After Reading Activities encourage students to reflect upon and respond to what they have read. A variety of creative activities integrate reading and writing and require students to think critically and creatively, use text structure, select main ideas, organize information, write summaries, apply what they have learned, and extend their learning and thinking.

Subject Area Activities focus on the demands of reading and learning specific subject content.

Strategy Evaluation Activities encourage students to think about their thinking and evaluate their reading and study strategies. The goal of these activities is to make students aware of their thinking and help them control it.

STRATEGY GUIDES

Strategy Guides provide a list of steps used by strategic readers when they apply specific reading and study strategies. The *Strategy Guides* are useful teaching aids to accompany strategy instruction and review. Students may use the *Strategy Guides* as references as they do the *Comprehension and Study Activities.*

• **enhances literature-based and whole language reading programs**.

> The generic nature of the *Comprehension and Study Activities* enables you to use them with any nonfiction text – trade books, periodicals, textbooks, and essays.

> The *Comprehension and Study Activities* are appropriate with any topic and may be used with nonfiction selections in thematic units or integrated curriculum units.

> The versatile nature of the *Comprehension and Study Activities* enables you to assign them to individuals reading different books, to a small group of students reading the same book, or to the entire class.

> The postreading activities integrate reading and writing and are especially useful for helping students write summaries.

> The *Strategy Guides* help you explain and model active reading strategies.

• **extends reading instruction across the curriculum**

> The *Comprehension and Study Activities* may be used across the curriculum with any subject area textbook.

> The *Comprehension and Study Activities* help students read and learn from their content area textbooks.

> The *Comprehension and Study Activities* and *Strategy Guides* enable you to teach reading and study strategies at the same time you impart your subject area content.

What Do You Know?

1 BEFORE YOU READ

Preview the selection.
- For an article or textbook chapter, read the title and bold headings.
- For a book, read the chapter titles.

Then answer the questions. Write your answers on the lines.

What is the topic of the selection? _____

What do you already know about this topic?

What do you know?

_____
_____
_____
_____
_____
_____
_____
_____
_____
_____
_____

Set your purpose. What do you want to know about this topic?

What do you want to know?

• _____
• _____
• _____
• _____
• _____
• _____

2 READ THE SELECTION

As you read, look for answers to your questions. Think about new information.

Activity – *Brainstorm and question*

Reading-Study Strategy   K-W-L

Comprehension Focus   activate prior knowledge
focus attention
set own purpose for reading

Writing Focus   write a list; formulate questions

Teaching Suggestions   This prereading activity is designed to be used alone or in conjunction with the postreading activity on page 3.

Remind students that a selection topic describes what the selection is generally about and is stated in one or two words. Use the **Previewing Strategy Guide** on page 99 to review how to preview a selection.

Have students who are reading the same book work in **cooperative groups** to share their background information and write questions they all have.

What Do You Know? (part 2)

3 **AFTER YOU READ**

What did you learn about the topic? On the notebook page, list new information and the answers to the questions you had before reading.

What I learned

NEW!

- _____
- _____
- _____
- _____
- _____
- _____
- _____
- _____
- _____
- _____
- _____
- _____
- _____
- _____
- _____
- _____

Put a star next to the facts that answer the questions you had before reading.

Is there anything you still want to know about the topic? Write three questions you have.

- _____
- _____
- _____

Where will you look to find the answers to your questions? _____

_____

Activity – *List new learning*

Reading-Study Strategy   K-W-L

Comprehension Focus   evaluate understanding
integrate new learning

Writing Focus   write a list; formulate questions

Teaching Suggestions   This postreading activity is designed to be used alone or as a follow-up to the prereading activity on page 1.

To provide practice using reference materials, have students work individually or in **cooperative groups** to find the answers to some of their questions.

To extend the activity, have students categorize or make a semantic map of the information they now know about the topic. Use **Sort It Out**, page 79, or **Think, Map and Read (part 2),** page 19, to help students organize their information.

Name _____

Title _____

Take Five

Preview the selection. What is its topic? _____

Write one or two paragraphs that tell everything you know about the topic. Write for five minutes. Use the back of the page if you need more space. As you write, you will have questions about the topic. Write them at the bottom of the page.

Write

Questions

-
-
-
-

2 READ THE SELECTION As you read, look for the answers to your questions.

Activity – *Write for five minutes*

Reading-Study Strategy   five-minute write

Comprehension Focus   activate prior knowledge
focus attention
set own purpose for reading

Writing Focus   write an explanation

Teaching Suggestions   This prereading activity is designed to be used alone or in conjunction with the postreading activity on page 7.

Explain to students that as they write about the topic, questions will come to their minds. These questions will help them set their purpose for reading.

Review that a selection topic describes what the selection is generally about. The topic is stated in one or two words. Use the ***Previewing Strategy Guide*** on page 99 to review how to preview a selection and the ***Setting the Purpose for Reading Strategy Guide*** on page 103 to review how to set one's purpose for reading.

Name

Title

Take Five (part 2)

3 AFTER YOU READ Look back at the questions you wrote before you read the selection. Put a check next to the ones that were answered in the selection. On the lines, write the answers to those questions. Look back through the selection if you wish.

Answers

-

-

-

-

-

What questions do you still have about the topic? List two.

- _____

- _____

Where can you look to find the answers to these questions?

_____

_____

Activity – *Answer purpose-setting questions*

Reading-Study Strategy

reflect upon what was read

Comprehension Focus

evaluate understanding
integrate new information

Writing Focus

write questions and answers

Teaching Suggestions

This postreading activity is designed to be used as a follow-up to the prereading activity on page 5.

To develop research skills and extend the postreading activity, have students use reference sources to find the answer to one of the questions they still have about the selection content.

Frame It!

1 BEFORE YOU READ

Preview the selection.
- For a textbook chapter, read the title, bold headings, and first and last paragraphs.
- For a book, read the chapter titles and the first paragraph of each chapter.

Then complete the paragraph frames.

After previewing the selection, I know that I will be reading about _____

_____ . One idea related to this topic that I think the writer will discuss is

_____ .

I also expect the writer will tell about _____

_____

_____ .

I already know some things about the topic. I know that _____

_____

_____

_____

_____

_____ .

Some of the things that I don't know about the topic but hope to learn about are

_____

_____

_____

_____

_____ .

2 READ THE SELECTION

As you read, look for the information you hope to learn. Also look for other new information the writer presents.

Activity – *Complete paragraph frames*

Reading-Study Strategy   preview and predict

Comprehension Focus   activate prior knowledge
focus attention
set own purpose for reading

Writing Focus   write paragraphs - main idea and supporting details

Teaching Suggestions   This prereading activity is designed to be used alone or in conjunction with the postreading activity on page 11.

Remind students that the topic describes what the selection is generally about and is stated in one or two words. Use the ***Previewing Strategy Guide*** on page 99 to review how to preview a selection.

Frame It! (part 2)

 **AFTER
YOU
READ**   Complete the paragraph frames.

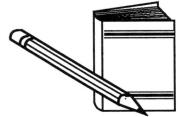

The selection is about _____ . The writer begins with _____

_____ .

The writer then discusses _____

_____ .

The writer also tells about _____

_____

_____

_____

_____

_____ .

I learned some things I didn't already know. For example, I learned that _____

_____

_____ .

Additionally, I learned _____

_____

_____

_____

_____ .

There are some things about the topic that I'd still like to know. First, _____

_____

_____ .

Also, I'd like to know _____

_____

_____

_____ .

Activity – Complete paragraph frames

Reading-Study Strategy   reflect on what was read

Comprehension Focus   select and organize main ideas
integrate new information
evaluate understanding

Writing Focus   write paragraphs – summary and main idea

Teaching Suggestions   This postreading activity is designed to be used alone or as a follow-up to the prereading activity on page 9.

To develop research skills, have students use reference sources to find information about one thing they still want to know about the topic.

Look Ahead - Think Back

1 BEFORE YOU READ

=== **Preview** ===

• For a textbook chapter or an article, read the title, bold headings, and the first and last paragraphs.

• For a book, read the chapter titles and the first paragraph of each chapter.

=== **Predict** ===

What is the topic of the selection? _____

What subtopics will the writer discuss? Write them on the lines.

• _____   • _____

• _____   • _____

• _____   • _____

• _____

Explain what you think you will learn from reading this selection. Write your predictions on the lines.

_____

_____

_____

_____

_____

_____

_____

_____

_____

_____

2 READ THE SELECTION

Read to see how closely your predictions match what the writer discusses.

Activity – *Make predictions*

Reading-Study Strategy   preview, predict, and confirm predictions

Comprehension Focus   activate prior knowledge
focus attention
set own purpose for reading

Writing Focus   write an explanation

Teaching Suggestions   This prereading activity is designed to be used alone or in conjunction with the postreading activity on page 15.

Remind students that a topic describes what the selection is generally about and is stated in one or two words. Explain that topics may be divided into smaller parts of information, or subtopics. Subtopics tell about the main topic.

Examples

Topic:	**Crocodiles**	**Lincoln**
Subtopics	characteristics	early life
	habitat	as a lawyer
	food	election of 1860
	enemies	as President

Explain to students that previewing and predicting will help them more easily read and understand a selection. Use the **Previewing Strategy Guide** on page 99 to review how to preview a selection. You may also wish to review purpose-setting with students. See the **Setting the Purpose Strategy Guide** on page 103.

Look Ahead - Think Back

3 **AFTER YOU READ**

Confirm

Complete the map with new information you learned from the selection. Choose four subtopics that the writer discusses. Write the subtopics on the lines next to the numbers. Under each subtopic, write two facts that you learned about the subtopic.

1 _____

■ _____   ■ _____

_____   _____

2 _____

■ _____   ■ _____

_____   _____

3 _____

■ _____   ■ _____

_____   _____

4 _____

■ _____   ■ _____

_____   _____

NEW!

✓ How close were your predictions? Explain your answer.

_____

_____

_____

_____

_____

_____

Activity – *Map new information*

Reading-Study Strategy   preview, predict, and confirm

Comprehension Focus   confirm predictions
select and organize information
integrate new information

Writing Focus   write a paragraph of explanation

Teaching Suggestions   This postreading activity is designed to be used alone or as a follow-up to the prereading activity on page 13. If you choose to use the activity alone, have students skip the last question.

Think, Map and Read

Preview the selection to find its topic. Write the topic in the oval. On the lines, write what you already know about the topic. Cluster your information around the oval. Then follow the directions to organize the information.

Organize the information in your cluster. Use the back of this page for your work.

• First, sort the information into categories, or groups of related facts.

• Then title each category. The title should tell what the group of facts is generally about.

Put the information onto the map in part 2 of this activity.

Activity – *Brainstorm and categorize*

Reading-Study Strategy   brainstorm and categorize

Comprehension Focus   activate background knowledge
organize information

Teaching Suggestions   This prereading activity is designed to be used in conjunction with the activity on page 19.

Remind students that the topic describes what the selection is generally about and is stated in one or two words. Use the *Previewing Strategy Guide* on page 99 to review how to preview a selection.

Some students may need instruction in categorizing information and labeling the categories.

Think, Map and Read (part 2)

Complete the map with the information from part 1 of the activity. Write the topic in the center. Write the category titles in the smaller ovals. Around each oval, write the information that goes in each category.

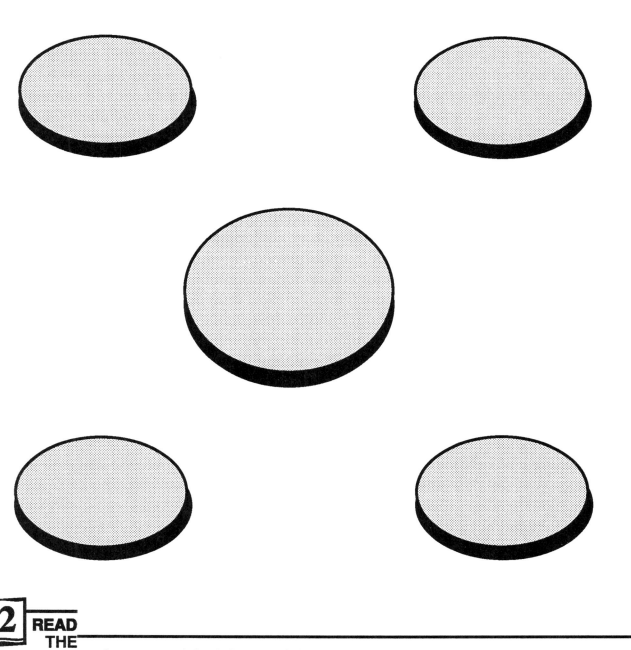

2 READ THE SELECTION   As you read, look for new information to add to your map.

3 AFTER YOU READ   Add new information from the selection to your map. Add new categories if you need them.

Activity – *Create a semantic map*

Reading-Study Strategy   semantic mapping

Comprehension Focus

set own purpose for reading
select and organize information
integrate new information with prior knowledge

Teaching Suggestions

This activity page is designed to be used in conjunction with the activity on page 17.

To develop **speaking skills**, have students use their maps to give short book talks about their selections. Explain that in their book talks, students should summarize the selection content and make a recommendation about whether classmates should read the book.

If students have used a content area textbook for this activity, point out that they can use their completed maps to review for a test.

Ask a Good Question

1 BEFORE YOU READ

Read the selection title. What questions come to your mind? Set your purpose for reading by writing five questions. Use the words below to begin your questions.

| who | what | when | where | why | how | will I |

1. _____

2. _____

3. _____

4. _____

5. _____

2 READ THE SELECTION

As you read, keep your questions in mind. Look for their answers.

3 AFTER YOU READ

Answer your questions. Go back to the selection if you wish.

1. _____
   _____

2. _____
   _____

3. _____
   _____

4. _____
   _____

5. _____
   _____

Activity – *Generate and answer questions*

Reading-Study Strategy   self-questioning guide

Comprehension Focus   activate prior knowledge
set own purpose for reading
integrate new information
check understanding

Writing Focus   write questions and answers

Teaching Suggestions   When assigning this activity, check that the selection title gives enough information to enable students to generate questions which will guide their reading.

Explain to students that they should write questions which they want answered in the selection. Encourage students to personalize their questions by using "I" and "me." Use the question stems to model the types of question students should generate.

> Example
>
> Selection Title: *Creatures of the Night Waters*
> - What kind of creatures will I read about?
> - Why are these creatures important enough to write a book about?
> - Who studies these creatures?
> - Will I find these creatures interesting?
> - What do these creatures do during the day?

Name _____

Title _____

Ask First

1 BEFORE YOU READ

Preview the selection.
- For a textbook chapter or an article, read the title, bold headings, and the first and last paragraphs.
- For a book, read the chapter titles and the first paragraph of each chapter.

Predict and Set Your Purpose

What is the topic of the selection? _____

Write six questions that you expect to be answered in the selection. Write your questions on the lines.

1 ▢ _____
_____

2 ▢ _____
_____

3 ▢ _____
_____

4 ▢ _____
_____

5 ▢ _____
_____

6 ▢ _____
_____

2 READ THE SELECTION

As you read the selection, look for the answers to your questions.
Put a **+** in the box if the question is answered in the selection.

3 AFTER YOU READ

On a separate sheet of paper, write the answers to the questions with a **+**.
Go back to the selection for help.

Activity – *Write and answer questions*

Reading-Study Strategy   self-questioning guide

Comprehension Focus   activate prior knowledge
set own purpose for reading
evaluate understanding

Writing Focus   write questions and answers

Teaching Suggestions   Remind students that the topic describes what the selection is generally about and is stated in one or two words. Use the *Previewing Strategy Guide* on page 99 to review how to preview a selection and the *Setting the Purpose Strategy Guide* on page 103 to review how to set one's purpose for reading.

To extend the activity and to provide practice using reference materials, have students use a variety of sources to find the answers to questions that were not answered in the selection. Students may work independently to answer one or two questions or in *cooperative groups* to answer a number of questions.

To develop *speaking and listening skills*, have students present their findings to the class.

Name _____

Title _____

Before
or
Vocabulary
After
Reading

Use the Clues

Skim the selection to identify unfamiliar words.
Choose four to define. Follow the directions in
Step A to use context clues to figure out a word's
meaning. If there are no good clues, go to Step B.

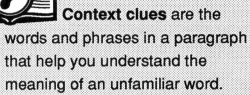

Context clues are the
words and phrases in a paragraph
that help you understand the
meaning of an unfamiliar word.

1   NEW WORD _____ PAGE _____

A   I CAN FIGURE OUT THE MEANING OF THE WORD FROM CONTEXT CLUES. THE WORD MEANS

_____

_____

TWO CLUES THAT I USED TO HELP ME DEFINE THE WORD ARE

• _____

• _____

B   THERE ARE NO GOOD CLUES TO HELP ME FIGURE OUT THE WORD'S MEANING. THEREFORE, I MUST

LOOK UP THE WORD IN THE DICTIONARY. THE DICTIONARY MEANING OF THE WORD IS

Dictionary

_____

2   NEW WORD _____ PAGE _____

A   I CAN FIGURE OUT THE MEANING OF THE WORD FROM CONTEXT CLUES. THE WORD MEANS

_____

_____

TWO CLUES THAT I USED TO HELP ME DEFINE THE WORD ARE

• _____

• _____

B   THERE ARE NO GOOD CLUES TO HELP ME FIGURE OUT THE WORD'S MEANING. THEREFORE, I MUST

LOOK UP THE WORD IN THE DICTIONARY. THE DICTIONARY MEANING OF THE WORD IS

Dictionary

_____

Activity – *Define new words*

Reading-Study Strategy   use contextual analysis

Comprehension Focus   provide background knowledge
expand vocabulary

Teaching Suggestions   This page is the first of a two-page vocabulary activity that continues on page 27.

This vocabulary activity may be used before reading to introduce students to unfamiliar words they will encounter in the selection or after reading to solidify their understanding of new words. Guide students to choose words that are key to understanding the selection.

Use the ***Understanding New Words*** and ***Using Context Clues Strategy Guides*** on pages 107 and 109 to review how to figure out the meaning of an unfamiliar word during reading.

Use the Clues (part 2)

Continue to define your new words.   Remember to follow the directions in Step A to use context clues to figure out a word's meaning. If there are no good clues, go to Step B.

3 **NEW WORD** _____ **PAGE** _____

A I CAN FIGURE OUT THE MEANING OF THE WORD FROM CONTEXT CLUES. THE WORD MEANS

_____

_____

TWO CLUES THAT I USED TO HELP ME DEFINE THE WORD ARE

● _____

● _____

B THERE ARE NO GOOD CLUES TO HELP ME FIGURE OUT THE WORD'S MEANING. THEREFORE, I MUST

LOOK UP THE WORD IN THE DICTIONARY. THE DICTIONARY MEANING OF THE WORD IS

_____

4 **NEW WORD** _____ **PAGE** _____

A I CAN FIGURE OUT THE MEANING OF THE WORD FROM CONTEXT CLUES. THE WORD MEANS

_____

_____

TWO CLUES THAT I USED TO HELP ME DEFINE THE WORD ARE

● _____

● _____

B THERE ARE NO GOOD CLUES TO HELP ME FIGURE OUT THE WORD'S MEANING. THEREFORE, I MUST

LOOK UP THE WORD IN THE DICTIONARY. THE DICTIONARY MEANING OF THE WORD IS

_____

_____

Activity – *Define new words*

Reading-Study Strategy   use contextual analysis

Comprehension Focus   provide background knowledge
expand vocabulary

Teaching Suggestions   This activity page is the second of a two-page vocabulary
activity that begins on page 25.

If you wish to have students define more than four words
from the selection, make additional copies of this page.

For Example

Choose three important words from the selection. Complete a vocabulary map for each one.

MEANING _____

_____

EXAMPLES   NON-EXAMPLES

_____   _____

_____   _____

_____   _____

MEANING _____

_____

EXAMPLES   NON-EXAMPLES

_____   _____

_____   _____

_____   _____

MEANING _____

_____

EXAMPLES   NON-EXAMPLES

_____   _____

_____   _____

_____   _____

Activity – *Complete word maps*

Reading-Study Strategy   examples and non-examples

Comprehension Focus   build background knowledge
apply word meanings
expand vocabulary

Teaching Suggestions   This vocabulary activity may be used before reading to introduce students to unfamiliar words they will encounter in the selection or after reading to solidify their understanding of new words. Guide students to choose words that are key to understanding the selection and for which examples and non-examples can be given.

Explain to students that one way to learn a new word is to give examples of things that illustrate its meaning and examples of things that do not illustrate it.
Example

glossy
meaning: smooth and shiny

Examples	Non-Examples
a pearl	skin of a peach
marble	rusted metal
satin	carpet

You may wish to have students do the activity in **cooperative groups**. Encourage students to justify their answers.

What's in a Word?

Skim the selection to identify unfamiliar words. Choose three important ones.
Complete a vocabulary map for each one. Use context clues and a dictionary.

Meaning _____

_____

(**Word**)

Example or picture

Sentence _____

_____

_____

Synonym _____

Meaning _____

_____

(**Word**)

Example or picture

Sentence _____

_____

_____

Synonym _____

Meaning _____

_____

(**Word**)

Example or picture

Sentence _____

_____

_____

Synonym _____

Activity – *Complete vocabulary maps*

Reading-Study Strategy   define and use new words

Comprehension Focus   build background knowledge
apply and use word meanings
expand vocabulary

Writing Focus   write sentences

Teaching Suggestions   This vocabulary activity may be used before reading to introduce students to unfamiliar words they will encounter in the selection or after reading to solidify their understanding of new words. Guide students to choose words that are key to understanding the selection. If you wish to have students define more than three words from the selection, make additional copies of this page.

Encourage students to draw on their own experiences to give examples that illustrate each word's meaning. Remind them that their sentences should indicate that they understand the meanings of the vocabulary words.

Have students work in **cooperative groups** to reinforce and apply word meanings. Each group will choose three words from their activity sheets to present to the class. Students will either act out a word's meaning or present a visual that illustrates it.

Words to Remember

Skim the selection to find unfamiliar words. Choose three that are important to understanding the selection. Use context clues and a dictionary to complete the paragraph frames about the words.

Dictionary

One word I don't know is _____. From clues in the sentences around the word, I think it means _____ _____. According to the dictionary, I'm *right / close / way off*. The dictionary meaning of the word is _____ _____.

A personal clue to help me remember the word is _____ _____.

Dictionary

One word I don't know is _____. From clues in the sentences around the word, I think it means _____ _____. According to the dictionary, I'm *right / close / way off*. The dictionary meaning of the word is _____ _____.

A personal clue to help me remember the word is _____ _____.

Dictionary

One word I don't know is _____. From clues in the sentences around the word, I think it means _____ _____. According to the dictionary, I'm *right / close / way off*. The dictionary meaning of the word is _____ _____.

A personal clue to help me remember the word is _____ _____.

Activity – *Complete paragraph frames*

Reading-Study Strategy

define new words

Comprehension Focus

use contextual analysis
build background knowledge
relate word meaning to personal experience
expand vocabulary

Writing Focus

complete paragraph frames

Teaching Suggestions

This vocabulary activity may be used before reading to introduce students to unfamiliar words they will encounter in the selection or after reading to solidify their understanding of new words. Guide students to choose words that are key to understanding the selection. If you wish to have students learn more than three words from the selection, make additional copies of this page.

Use the **Understanding New Words** and **Using Context Clues Strategy Guides** on pages 107 and 109 to review how to figure out the meaning of an unfamiliar word during reading.

Explain that a personal clue is something from the student's own life that he or she associates with the word. For example, a personal clue for *dilapidated* may be an abandoned building next to the record store that the student frequents. Tell students that a personal clue helps a person remember a word by linking its meaning to something he or she already knows.

Name _____

Title _____

Before
or
Vocabulary
After
Reading

Connect Words

Follow the dirctions to complete the vocabulary overview.

1 Write the selection topic on the line.

2 Skim the selection to find four unfamiliar words that are related to the topic.

3 Write the words at the top of each word map.

4 Write your own definition for each word. Use context clues in the text to develop your definition. Use a dictionary if you need help.

5 Write a personal clue under each word. To write a personal clue, think about the word's meaning. Connect the word to something you know.

TOPIC: _____

WORD: _____

PERSONAL CLUE

DEFINITION

WORD: _____

PERSONAL CLUE

DEFINITION

WORD: _____

PERSONAL CLUE

DEFINITION

WORD: _____

PERSONAL CLUE

DEFINITION

Activity – *Complete a vocabulary overview*

Reading-Study Strategy   define and use new words

Comprehension Focus

build background knowledge
relate word meaning to personal experience
expand vocabulary

Writing Focus   write definitions

Teaching Suggestions

This vocabulary activity may be used before reading to introduce students to unfamiliar words they will encounter in the selection or after reading to solidify their understanding of new words.

You may want to help students identify the category, or topic, and then guide them to choose words that are related to the topic and also key to understanding the selection.

Encourage students to formulate their own definitions. Use the **Understanding New Words** and **Using Context Clues Strategy Guides** on page 107 and 109 to review how to develop word meanings.

Explain to students that a personal clue is something from the student's own life that he or she associates with the word. For example, a personal clue for *murky* might be the water in a mud puddle near the student's home. Explain that a personal clue helps a person remember a word by linking its meaning to something he or she already knows.

Just Checking

Divide the selection into four parts. Write the page numbers of each part at the top of each box. Follow the directions to read each part of the selection. Write your answers on the lines.

PART 1 pages ____ to ____

1 PREVIEW - PREDICT

Preview part 1. Read the bold headings or the first sentence in each paragraph.
What will you read about in this part of the selection?

_____

_____

2 READ PART 1

3 CHECK UNDERSTANDING

What did you read about in this section? List the important ideas.   If you cannot list these ideas, reread the material. Then list them.

_____

_____

PART 2 pages ____ to ____

1 PREVIEW - PREDICT

Preview part 2. Read the bold headings or the first sentence in each paragraph.
What will you read about in this part of the selection?

_____

_____

2 READ PART 2

3 CHECK UNDERSTANDING

What did you read about in this section? List the important ideas. If you cannot list these ideas, reread the material. Then list them.

_____

_____

Activity – *Monitor comprehension*

Reading-Study Strategy   predict – read – summarize

Comprehension Focus   set own purpose for reading
check understanding during reading
use fix-up strategies

Teaching Suggestions   This page is the first of a two-page comprehension monitoring guide that continues on page 39. If you wish to
have students divide a selection into more than four parts,
make additional copies of page 39.

Explain to students that the purpose of this activity is to
help them think as they read. Good readers continually
monitor their comprehension. They make predictions
about what they will read and then stop to confirm their
predictions and summarize important ideas. When good
readers realize that understanding has failed, they take
remedial action. Use the *Monitoring Comprehension
Strategy Guide* on page 105 to review how good readers
monitor their comprehension and to discuss the fix-up
strategies good readers use.

Use the *Previewing Strategy Guide* on page 99 to
review how to preview a selection.

Students may do this guided reading activity in
cooperative groups. Have students work together to do
Steps 1 and 3, but have them do the reading in Step 2
independently. If students disagree about the important
ideas, they should all reread to check their understanding.

Just Checking (part 2)

Follow the directions to read the rest of the selection.

PART 3 pages ____ to ____

1 PREVIEW - PREDICT

Preview part 3. Read the bold heading or the first sentence in each paragraph.
What will you read about in this part of the selection?

_____

_____

2 READ PART 3

3 CHECK UNDERSTANDING

What did you read about? List the important ideas. If you cannot list these ideas, reread
the material. Then list them.

_____

_____

PART 4 pages ____ to ____

1 PREVIEW - PREDICT

Review the last section. Read the bold headings or the first sentence in each paragraph.
What will you read about in this part of the selection?

_____

_____

2 READ PART 4

3 CHECK UNDERSTANDING

What did you read about? List the important ideas. If you cannot list these ideas, reread
the material. Then list them.

_____

_____

Activity – *Monitor comprehension*

Reading-Study Strategy   predict – read – summarize

Comprehension Focus   set own purpose for reading
check understanding during reading
use fix-up strategies

Teaching Suggestions   This page is the second of a two-page comprehension
monitoring guide that begins on page 37. If you wish to
have students divide the selection into more than four
parts, make additional copies of this page.

After students complete the selection, have them discuss
how using this monitoring guide affected their comprehension. Encourage students to verbalize the thinking processes they used as they read and to describe what they
did when they found that they didn't understand a passage.

Stop and Think

Divide the selection into four parts. Then follow the directions to read each part. Write the answers to questions on the lines.

Predict   Begin by reading the selection title and its first paragraph.
What will you read about in the first part of the selection?

_____

_____

Read   As you read, think about what the writer says. See if it is what you expect.

Confirm   What does the writer discuss? Is it what you predicted?
If you cannot answer the questions, reread the section. Then answer them.

_____

_____

↓

Predict   Based on what you know now, what predictions can you make about what you will read next?

_____

_____

Read   As you read, think about what the writer says. See if it is what you expect.

Confirm   What does the writer discuss? Is it what you predicted?
If you cannot answer the questions, reread the section. Then answer them.

_____

_____

↓

Activity – *Monitor comprehension*

Reading-Study Strategy   predict – read – confirm

Comprehension Focus   set own purpose for reading
check understanding during reading
use fix-up strategies

Teaching Suggestions   This page is the first of a two-page comprehension monitoring guide that continues on page 43. If you wish to have
students divide a selection into more than four parts, make
additional copies of page 43.

Explain to students that the purpose of this activity is to
help them think as they read. Good readers continually
monitor their comprehension. They make predictions
about what they will read and then stop to confirm their
predictions and summarize important ideas. When good
readers realize that understanding has failed, they take
remedial action. Use the **Monitoring Comprehension
Strategy Guide** on page 105 to review how good readers
monitor their comprehension and to discuss the fix-up
strategies good readers use.

Students may do this guided reading activity in
cooperative groups. Have students work together to do
Steps 1 and 3, but have them do the reading in Step 2
independently. If students disagree about the important
ideas, they should all reread to check their understanding.

Stop and Think (part 2)

Follow the directions to read the rest of the selection.

Predict Based on what you know now, what predictions can you make about what you will read next?

_____

_____

Read As you read, think about what the writer says. See if it is what you expect.

Confirm What does the writer discuss? Is it what you predicted?
If you cannot answer the questions, reread the section. Then answer them.

_____

_____

↓

Predict Based on what you know now, what predictions can you make about what you will read next?

_____

_____

Read As you read, think about what the writer says. See if it is what you expect.

Confirm What does the writer discuss? Is it what you predicted?
If you cannot answer the questions, reread the section. Then answer them.

_____

_____

Evaluate your reading and thinking

How did using this guide help you better understand and read the selection?

_____

_____

Activity – *Monitor comprehension*

Reading-Study Strategy   predict – read – confirm

Comprehension Focus   set own purpose for reading
check understanding during reading
use fix-up strategies
evaluate thinking and reading strategies

Teaching Suggestions   This page is the second of a two-page comprehension monitoring guide that begins on page 41. If you wish to have students divide the selection into more than four parts, make additional copies of this page.

After students complete the selection, have them discuss how using this monitoring guide affected their comprehension. Encourage students to verbalize the thinking processes they used as they read and to describe what they did when they found that they didn't understand a passage.

Stay Tuned

Divide the selection into four sections. Write the section page numbers in the corner of each box. Then follow the directions to read each section. Write question answers on the lines.

SECTION 1   pages _____ - _____

Predict

Read the bold headings or read the first sentence of each paragraph.
What is the topic of this section? _____

Read

As you read Section 1, *think* about what the writer says about the topic.

Summarize

What are the most important ideas about the topic? Explain them in two
or three sentences.   If you cannot state the important ideas, reread the
section. Then answer the question.

_____

_____

_____

SECTION 2   pages _____ - _____

Predict

Read the bold headings or read the first sentence of each paragraph.
What is the topic of this section? _____

Read

As you read Section 2, *think* about what the writer says about the topic.

Summarize

What are the most important ideas about the topic? Explain them in two
or three sentences.   If you cannot state the important ideas, reread the
section. Then answer the question.

_____

_____

_____

Activity – *Monitor comprehension*

Reading-Study Strategy   predict – read – summarize

Comprehension Focus   set own purpose for reading
check understanding during reading
use fix-up strategies

Teaching Suggestions   This page is the first of a two-page comprehension monitoring guide that continues on page 47. If you wish to
have students divide a selection into more than four parts,
make additional copies of page 47.

Explain to students that the purpose of this activity is to
help them think as they read. Good readers continually
monitor their comprehension. They make predictions
about what they will read and then stop to confirm their
predictions and summarize important ideas. When good
readers realize that understanding has failed, they take
remedial action. Use the ***Monitoring Comprehension
Strategy Guide*** on page 105 to review how good readers
monitor their comprehension and to discuss the fix-up
strategies good readers use.

Students may do this guided reading activity in
cooperative groups. Have students work together to do
Steps 1 and 3, but have them do the reading in Step 2
independently. If students disagree about the important
ideas, they should all reread to check their understanding.

Stay Tuned (part 2)

Continue reading.   Follow the directions to read each section. Write question answers on the lines.

SECTION 3   pages _____ - _____

Predict

Read the bold headings or read the first sentence of each paragraph.
What is the topic of this section? _____

Read

As you read Section 3, *think* about what the writer says about the topic.

Summarize

What are the most important ideas about the topic? Explain them in two
or three sentences.   If you cannot state the important ideas, reread the
section. Then answer the question.

_____

_____

_____

SECTION 4   pages _____ - _____

Predict

Read the bold headings or read the first sentence of each paragraph.
What is the topic of this section? _____

Read

As you read Section 4, *think* about what the writer says about the topic.

Summarize

What are the most important ideas about the topic? Explain them in two
or three sentences.   If you cannot state the important ideas, reread the
section. Then answer the question.

_____

_____

_____

Activity – *Monitor comprehension*

Reading-Study Strategy   predict – read – summarize

Comprehension Focus   set own purpose for reading
check understanding during reading
use fix-up strategies

Teaching Suggestions   This page is the second of a two-page comprehension monitoring guide that begins on page 45. If you wish to have students divide the selection into more than four parts, make additional copies of this page.

After students complete the selection, have them discuss how using this monitoring guide affected their comprehension. Encourage students to verbalize the thinking processes they used as they read and to describe what they did when they found that they didn't understand a passage.

Take Note!

Take notes as you read. Write main ideas and key words in the left column. In the right column, write details and examples that explain main ideas and definitions of key terms.

Main Ideas / Key Words	Details / Examples / Definitions

Activity – *Take reading notes*

Reading-Study Strategy   note-taking

Comprehension Focus   select and organize main ideas and supporting details
use text structure to aid understanding
check understanding during reading
integrate new information

Writing Focus   take notes

Teaching Suggestions   Explain to students how to use the two-column note format: list main ideas and key terms in the left column; list important facts and examples that support and explain those ideas and terms next to them and down the right column. Use the *Taking Notes Strategy Guide* on page 115 to review how to take notes.

To take notes successfully, students must understand how writers develop main ideas and how to select those ideas. Use the *Finding Main Idea Strategy Guides,* pages 111 and 113, to teach and review finding main ideas.

Suggest that students use the two-column note format to take notes in all their classes. Tell them how to use two-column notes to study for tests: formulate questions from the information in one column; cover up the information in the other column and test yourself.

Write On

A cinquain is a five-line poem that follows a special form. Study the form and the examples. Then write a cinquain about one of the topics in the selection.

Pyramids	◀ one word title ▶	**Crocodiles**
Massive, Ancient	◀ two-word description ▶	**Thick-skinned, Scaly**
Preserving, Protecting, Honoring	◀ three words expressing action ▶	**Hunted, Slaughtered, Sold**
Built for Egyptian pharaohs	◀ four-word phrase that describes the topic ▶	**Valued for their hides**
Tombs	◀ one word that restates the topic ▶	**Endangered**

Plan your cinquain.

Choose a topic. Your topic will be your one-word title.

Topic: _____

On the back of this page, make four lists of words and phrases you might use to write your cinquain. Use the titles below for your lists.

descriptive words　　　**action words**　　　**four-word phrases**　　　**words related to the topic**

Write your cinquain. Follow the form above. Use some of your words and phrases.

_____

_____ _____

_____ _____ _____

_____

_____

Revise and edit your cinquain. Write the final copy on separate paper.

Activity – *Write a cinquain*

Reading-Study Strategy   reflect on what was read

Comprehension Focus   synthesize information
extend understanding

Writing Focus   write a poem

Teaching Suggestions   Have students prepare the final copies of their poems for display on a bulletin board of students' work. Some students may enjoy illustrating their cinquains.

If students read the same selection, you may wish to have them work in *cooperative groups* to write a progressive cinquain. Begin by assigning the topic for their cinquains. (Students still choose their own titles.) Have students write cinquains individually. Then have them work in pairs to produce a new cinquain either by combining the ones they have or by writing a new one. Next have two pairs combine and integrate their cinquains into a newly-created one. The recorders for the groups of four write the final cinquains on the chalkboard. The class then discusses how each one reflects new learning and understanding of the topic.

Name _____

Title _____

Get the Gist

Complete the map. First, write the topic of the selection in the center. Next, decide the five most important ideas the author discusses. Write one idea in each box.

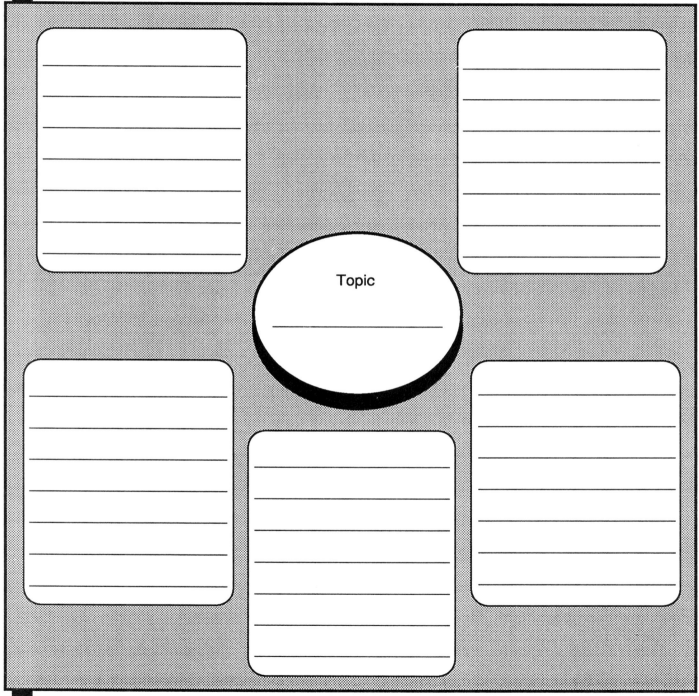

Topic

 On a separate sheet of paper, write a summary of the selection. Use the ideas in your map.

Activity – *Complete a map*

Reading-Study Strategy   identify and use text structure

Comprehension Focus   select main ideas
integrate new information

Writing Focus   write a summary

Teaching Suggestions   A prerequisite skill for summarizing is selecting main ideas and distinguishing them from details. Use the ***Finding the Main Idea Strategy Guides*** on pages 111 and 113 to review how to identify main ideas.

Use the ***Writing a Summary Strategy Guide*** on page 117 to review the steps for writing a summary.

Say It in a Sentence

Follow the directions to write a one-sentence summary of the selection.

Select Information

What is the topic of the selection? _____

What are the important ideas the writer discusses? List them.

- _____
- _____
- _____
- _____
- _____
- _____

Organize Information

Reread your list above.

- Write a **B** next to the idea with which the writer begins.
- Write an **M** next to the important ideas that the writer develops in the body of the selection.
- Write an **E** next to the idea with which the writer ends.

Write a One-Sentence Summary

The writer begins the selection with _____

_____, then

discusses _____

_____

_____

_____,

and ends with _____

_____.

Activity – *Write a one-sentence summary*

Reading-Study Strategy   summarize

Comprehension Focus   select and organize main ideas
integrate new information

Writing Focus   write a summary

Teaching Suggestions   A prerequisite skill for summarizing is selecting main ideas and distinguishing them from details. Use the ***Finding the Main Idea Strategy Guides*** on pages 111 and 113 to review how to identify main ideas.

Use the ***Writing a Summary Strategy Guide*** on page 117 to review the steps for writing a summary.

To develop ***speaking skills***, have students read aloud their sentences.

Write It Down

Write a journal entry in which you discuss your personal reaction to the selection. Choose one of the topics below or think of one of your own.

- what you liked or didn't like about the selection and why
- why you do or do not agree with the writer's opinions
- how you can use the information in the selection in your own life

DATE: _____

TOPIC: _____

_____
_____
_____
_____
_____
_____
_____
_____
_____
_____
_____
_____
_____
_____
_____
_____
_____
_____
_____
_____
_____
_____

Activity – *Write a journal entry*

Reading-Study Strategy   think critically

Comprehension Focus   evaluate selection content
apply new learning

Writing Focus   write a personal reaction

Teaching Suggestions   If you wish to have students write daily or weekly reactions
to selections they are reading, make additional copies of
this activity page.

What's It All About?

Follow the steps to plan and write a summary of
the selection.

> **A summary** retells
> the most important
> ideas in a selection.

1 Complete the chart.

TOPIC _____	
Main Ideas (important ideas that tell about the topic)	**Important Details**

2 Do each step in the checklist. As you do a task, put a check in the box.

Checklist

Reread the information above.

☐ Check that you chose the most important ideas.

☐ Cross out unimportant information.

☐ Cross out ideas that repeat.

☐ Look for places where a one-word label can replace several items.

    Example: *Silverware* replaces *knife, fork, and spoon.*

Activity – Write a summary

Reading-Study Strategy   summarize

Comprehension Focus   select and organize main ideas
integrate new information

Writing Focus   write a summary

Teaching Suggestions   This activity page is the first of a two-page summarizing activity that is designed to be used in conjunction with page 61.

A prerequisite skill for summarizing is selecting main ideas and distinguishing them from details. Use the *Finding the Main Idea Strategy Guides* on pages 111 and 113 to review how to identify main ideas.

Use the *Writing a Summary Strategy Guide* on page 117 to review the steps in writing a summary.

Point out that the details students include must be integral in explaining a main idea. Often there are no details important enough to be included in a summary.

If students have read the same selection, you may wish to have them work in *cooperative groups* to plan and write their summaries.

What's It All About? (part 2)

Follow the steps to organize and write your summary.

3 Put the information in the chart into sentences.
Write a sentence that states the topic.

* _____

_____

Write a sentence that states each main idea. Include details that go with an idea.

* _____

_____

* _____

_____

* _____

_____

4 Write your summary. Use your sentences. Use the back of the page for more space.

_____

_____

_____

_____

_____

_____

_____

_____

_____

_____

Revise and edit your summary. Check that your summary tells only the most important ideas in the selection. Write the final copy on separate paper.

Activity – *Write a summary*

Reading-Study Strategy   summarize

Comprehension Focus   select and organize main ideas
integrate new information

Writing Focus   write a summary

Teaching Suggestions   This page is the second of a two-page summarizing activity that is designed to be used in conjunction with the first part on page 59.

Short and to the Point

Imagine that your job is to write summaries for the jackets of books. Your boss has asked you to write a summary of the selection you just read. Follow the directions in A, B, and C.

A. On the line, write the selection topic.

_____

List 15 words that are related to the topic.

_____

_____

_____

_____

_____

_____

_____

_____

_____

_____

_____

_____

_____

_____

_____

Circle the words that are related to the most important ideas in the selection.

B. Write your summary on the flap of the book jacket. Include the words you circled. Use the back of this page if you need more space.

C. Revise and edit your summary. Write the final copy on separate paper.

Activity – *Write book jacket copy*

Reading-Study Strategy   summarize

Comprehension Focus

select and organize main ideas
integrate new information

Writing Focus

write a summary

Teaching Suggestions

To successfully summarize, students must be able to select main ideas and distinguish them from details. Use the ***Finding the Main Idea Strategy Guides*** on pages 111 and 113 to review how to identify main ideas. Tell students that in this exercise they should look for words that relate to main ideas.

Use the ***Writing a Summary Strategy Guide*** on page 117 to review the steps for writing a summary.

To develop ***speaking and listening skills,*** have students use their summaries to give short book talks.

What's New?

Write the answers to the questions on the lines.

What is the most important idea that the writer tells about in the selection?

What did you learn about this idea?

Imagine you are talking to a good friend. Explain to him or her how you can use what you learned in your everyday life.

Activity – *Tell a friend*

Reading-Study Strategy   reflect on what was read

Comprehension Focus   select main idea
integrate new information
apply new learning

Writing Focus   write an explanation

Teaching Suggestions   Have students work in **cooperative groups** to present
their new information. Challenge each group to think of an
innovative way to convey the ideas they learned from their
selections.   Students need not have read the same book
to work together.

Just the Facts

Imagine that you are a reporter who witnessed one of the events discussed in the reading. Write a news story to tell what happened. Remember that the lead paragraph of a news story tells the important facts – who, what, when, where, and why. The paragraphs that follow relate details about what happened. The headline states the main idea.

SPECIAL EDITION!   THE **NewsPaper**   **Read All About It!**

Revise and edit your news story. Write the final copy on separate paper.

Activity – Write a news story

Reading-Study Strategy   reflect on what was read

Comprehension Focus   select and organize important information
integrate new information

Writing Focus   write a news story
write from a different point of view

Teaching Suggestions   To extend the activity, have students create their own newspaper front pages on large paper. First they will write the final copies of their stories on the page. Then direct students to write two or three additional news stories related to their selections and add them to their front pages. Some students may wish to illustrate one of their stories. Display the newspaper pages on a bulletin board of students' work.

A Quick Review

Imagine that you are a book reviewer for school librarians. Write a review of the book you just read. In your review, tell what the book is about, who would enjoy reading it, and whether the librarian should purchase it. Support your opinions with facts and examples.

Organize your ideas by completing the chart.

Book Title _____

Author _____

Key ideas that tell what the book is about	Opinions	Support
	Who should read the book?	
	Should the librarian purchase the book?	

Write your review on separate paper. Use the information in your chart.

Activity – *Write a book review*

Reading-Study Strategy   read critically

Comprehension Focus   select and organize main ideas
                               evaluate a selection

Writing Focus   write to persuade

Teaching Suggestions   Encourage students to use specific examples to support
                               their opinions.

                               To develop **speaking skills**, have students present their
                               reviews in a television commentary format.

It's a Matter of Opinion

What is the topic of the selection? _____

What opinions does the writer express about the topic? How does the writer prove his or her points? What facts or examples does the writer use to support those opinions? Complete the chart to answer the questions.

Opinions	Proof (facts and examples)
•	• • • •
•	• • • •
•	• • • •

Does the writer convince you? Complete part 2 of this activity to answer the question.

Activity – *Identify opinions*

Reading-Study Strategy think critically

Comprehension Focus identify opinions and supporting evidence
identify and use text organization

Teaching Suggestions This page is the first of a two-page postreading activity. It may be used alone or in conjunction with the second part of the activity on page 73.

Before assigning this activity, be sure that students are reading a selection in which the writer expresses opinions.

Explain that as students read, they should think about how well a writer supports his or her opinions. They should look for supporting evidence, judge the accuracy of the evidence, and note whether opposing arguments are omitted or included.

It's a Matter of Opinion (part 2)

What is your opinion? Does the writer convince you?

Complete the chart with your opinion and at least three ideas to support it.

Opinion	Proof (facts and examples)
• I **agree / disagree** with the writer about _____ _____ _____	• • •

Complete the paragraph frame.

Write a letter to the writer explaining why you do or do not agree with him or her.

_____

Dear _____ ,

    I _____ with you about _____

_____. One reason that I feel this way is

_____

_____.

Another reason is _____

_____

_____

Also, _____

_____

_____.

_____

_____

Activity – *Write a letter*

Reading-Study Strategy   think critically

Comprehension Focus   evaluate a writer's message
integrate new information

Writing Focus   write to persuade

Teaching Suggestions   This page is the second of a two-page postreading activity and is designed to be done in conjunction with the first page on page 71.

Recap the Highlights

Complete the map with the six most important events that the writer discusses. List the events in the order they happened in time.

EVENTS

EVENT 1 _____

EVENT 2 _____

EVENT 3 _____

EVENT 4 _____

EVENT 5 _____

EVENT 6 _____

On separate paper, write a summary of what happened. Use the ideas in the map.

Activity – Map events

Reading-Study Strategy   identify and use text structure

Comprehension Focus   select and sequence main events
integrate new information

Writing Focus   write a summary

Teaching Suggestions   To extend the activity and develop *speaking skills*, have students work in *cooperative groups* to present their summaries in a news broadcast format.

Is It Important?

On the left side of the paper, write three of the most important ideas that the writer discusses. On the right side, write the facts or examples that the writer gives to explain or support each main idea.

MAIN IDEA	SUPPORTING FACTS AND EXAMPLES
▣	▪ _____ _____ ▪ _____ _____ ▪ _____ _____
▣	▪ _____ _____ ▪ _____ _____ ▪ _____ _____
▣	▪ _____ _____ ▪ _____ _____ ▪ _____ _____

Activity – *Find main ideas*

Reading-Study Strategy   identify and use text structure

Comprehension Focus   select main ideas
organize information

Teaching Suggestions   For longer selections you may wish to have students focus on more than three main ideas. Make additional copies of this activity page.

Use the ***Finding Main Idea Strategy Guides*** on pages 111 and 113 to review how to identify main ideas.

To improve ***study skills***, suggest that students use this activity page format for taking notes. Use the ***Taking Notes Strategy Guide*** on page 115 to review how to take two-column notes.

Sort It Out

Follow the directions to list and categorize words from the selection.

The topic of the selection is _____.

1 On the lines below, list twenty words that relate to the topic.

_____	_____	_____	_____
_____	_____	_____	_____
_____	_____	_____	_____
_____	_____	_____	_____
_____	_____	_____	_____

2 Group the words in the list into categories. Write each group in one column. Then title each category. Write the titles on the lines. Use as many words from the list as possible. Add categories if necessary, or organize the words into fewer categories.

3 Choose one group of words. On a separate sheet of paper, write a paragraph to explain why you grouped those words together. Use all the words in the group in your paragraph.

Activity – *List and categorize*

Reading-Study Strategy   reflect on new information

Comprehension Focus

organize new information
integrate new learning

Writing Focus

write a paragraph of explanation

Teaching Suggestions

Remind students that the topic describes what the selection is generally about and is stated in one or two words. Explain that a category title is a word or phrase that describes how all the words in a group are related.

Remind students that they need not use all twenty words in their categories and that they may add categories or sort words into fewer than four categories.

If students have read the same selection, you may wish to have them do the activity in **cooperative groups**.

To extend the activity, have students categorize the words in one or two additional ways.

Eye Witness

Choose an event from the selection. Imagine that you are a person who witnessed the event. Write a journal entry for that day. Describe the event. Then describe those thoughts and feelings you have about it.

JOURNAL ENTRY FOR _____, 19 _____

Activity – *Write a journal entry*

Reading-Study Strategy   reflect on what was read

Comprehension Focus   integrate new information
summarize

Writing Focus   write a personal reaction
write from different point of view

Teaching Suggestions   Review with students that in personal journals, people express their thoughts and feelings. Remind them that they are to imagine that they are someone who witnessed the event and write from the perspective of that person.

Name _____

Title _____

A Current Event

Read <u>two</u> or more news articles about a current issue. Then complete the map. Write the answers to the questions on the lines.

SPECIAL EDITION!   THE NewsPaper   Read All About It!

What is the problem?

_____

_____

What are the causes of the problem?

_____

_____

_____

_____

_____

_____

So far, what are the effects?

_____

_____

_____

What other effects are expected?

_____

_____

Imagine that you are given the job of solving the problem. What is one solution you would suggest? Explain what your solution is and why you think it is a good one.

_____

_____

_____

_____

_____

_____

_____

_____

_____

Activity – *Analyze a current issue*

Reading-Study Strategy   think critically

Comprehension Focus   integrate new information
identify causes and effects
solve problems

Writing Focus   write a paragraph of explanation

Teaching Suggestions   Students may do this activity in **cooperative groups**.
Direct each group member to read a different article from a
different periodical about the same issue. After completing
the top part of the map with the problem, causes, and
effects, have students brainstorm possible solutions.
Once the group arrives at a consensus about the best
solution, have them complete the last part of the activity.

No Problem!

Choose a math problem from your most recent assignment. Write a memo to a classmate that explains how you solved the problem. Begin your memo by showing the problem in the box. Then write your explanation on the lines.

Memo

To: _____

From: _____

$$3 \times 4 = ?$$

$$1 + 1 = 2$$

$$10 - 5 = 5$$

Problem:

Revise and edit your memo. Write the final copy on separate paper.

Activity – *Write a memo*

Reading-Study Strategy   reflect upon what was learned

Comprehension Focus   integrate and apply new learning
organize information into a sequence of steps

Writing Focus   write a how-to paragraph

Teaching Suggestions   For *prewriting* planning and organizing, have students list the steps they took to solve the problem and put the steps in the correct order.

Have students work in pairs to **revise and edit** their memos. Students exchange papers, follow the steps to work the problems, and give each other feedback about how to revise the memos for clarity.

Put It into Words

1 Choose one computational problem from a recent math assignment. Write the problem in the circle.

2 Turn the problem into a word problem. Write your word problem on the lines.

_____
_____
_____
_____
_____
_____
_____
_____
_____
_____
_____
_____
_____
_____
_____
_____
_____
_____
_____
_____
_____
_____

Math

3 Have a classmate solve your word problem.

Activity – *Write a word problem*

Reading-Study Strategy   reflect on new information

Comprehension Focus   apply new learning
check understanding

Writing Focus   write a word problem

Teaching Suggestions   As a ***prewriting activity***, have students list in order the operations necessary to solve the problem.

<u>Example</u>

$2 \times 7 - 3 = 11$

multiply   (2 times 7)

subtract   (3)

Have students use the steps to write their word problems.

To develop ***speaking and listening skills***, have students read aloud their problems and have the class or math group solve them.

Buy It

Write a letter to the director of an art museum. Convince the director to purchase a piece of art that you just read about and particularly like.

In your letter,

- state your request and describe the piece of art, and
- give at least three good reasons why the museum should buy the piece of art.

ARTSY MAGAZINE

_____

_____

Dear _____ ,

_____

_____

_____

_____

_____

_____

_____

_____

_____

_____

_____

_____

_____

_____

_____

_____

_____

_____

_____

_____

_____

Activity – Write a letter

Reading-Study Strategy   think critically

Comprehension Focus   integrate new information
evaluate selection content

Writing Focus   write to persuade

Teaching Suggestions   Encourage students to use specific details and examples to support their opinions.

As a **prewriting activity**, have students plan their letters on the back of the activity page. Suggest that they organize their letters into two paragraphs: one that describes the piece of art and one that gives reasons why the museum should purchase it. Have students make a map similar to the one below and add the information they want to include in their letters.

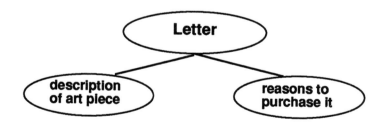

Dear John

Imagine that you are the scientist who just successfully conducted an experiment described in the selection. Write a letter to a good friend. Explain how you did the experiment and describe your results.

Dear _____ ,

Activity – *Write a friendly letter*

Reading-Study Strategy   reflect on what was read

Comprehension Focus   integrate new learning
summarize information

Writing Focus   write an explanation
write from a different point of view

Teaching Suggestions   As a **prewriting activity**, have students plan their letters on the back of the activity page. Suggest that students organize their letters into two paragraphs: (1) an explanation of how the experiment was done and (2) the results. Before writing their first paragraphs, have students list the steps they took to do the experiment.

Remind students that they are to put themselves in the place of the scientist and write from his or her point of view.

To extend the activity, have students assume the role of the friend and respond to the scientist's letter.

Name _____

Title _____

Sell It

Choose an idea, invention, or discovery discussed in your science textbook. Imagine that the idea, invention, or discovery is brand new. You are an advertising specialist who sells the public on new scientific ideas, inventions, and discoveries.

Create an advertisement which

- describes or shows the idea, invention, or discovery
- shows or explains how it helps people in their everyday lives

Use both illustrations and words.

Revise and edit your ad. Write and draw your final copy on separate paper.

Activity – *Create an advertisement*

Reading-Study Strategy   reflect on what was read

Comprehension Focus   apply new learning
select main ideas

Writing Focus   write to persuade

Teaching Suggestions   To develop *speaking skills*, have students present their advertisements as radio or television commercials.

Display the advertisements on a bulletin board of students' work.

How Did It Go?

How do you rate your general understanding of the selection? Circle your rating.

NOT GOOD　　　　　　OKAY　　　　　　GREAT →

1　　　**2**　　　**3**　　　**4**　　　**5**

Write a note to your teacher that explains your rating.

In the first paragraph, discuss one of the topics below.

- what made the reading easy or difficult
- what parts of the selection you didn't understand and why
- what you did in your head to read and understand the selection

In the last paragraph, explain what you will do the same or different next time you read.

Dear _____ ,

　　I gave myself a rating of _____ because _____

_____

_____

_____

_____

_____

_____

_____

_____

_____

_____

　　Next time I read a similar selection, I will _____

_____

_____

_____

_____

Activity – *Write a note*

Reading-Study Strategy   reflect on thinking

Comprehension Focus   evaluate understanding
evaluate own strategic reading

Writing Focus   write paragraphs of explanation

Teaching Suggestions   To help students think about their own reading strategies before they begin the activity, review the strategies good readers use to read and understand text – previewing, predicting, recalling background knowledge, skimming, self-questioning, reading for main ideas, using text structure, and periodic self-review. Use the ***Comprehension Monitoring Strategy Guide*** on page 105 to review how good readers check understanding and take remedial action when comprehension fails.

After students complete the activity, conduct a ***strategy conference*** in which students share their reading-thinking strategies. During the discussion, encourage students to explain which strategies worked well for them, which strategies might have helped them more, and which strategies they used when their comprehension failed.

Name _____

Title _____

**After
Reading**
Strategy
Evaluation

Think About Your Thinking

Think about how you read the selection and how well you understood it. Then follow the directions to answer the questions.

What did you do in your head that helped you read and understand the selection?
Check the boxes next to the strategies you used.

Before I read, I ...

- ☐ thought about what I already knew about topic
- ☐ predicted what the selection would be about
- ☐ asked myself questions about the selection topic
- ☐ read the title and bold headings
- ☐ skimmed the selection
- ☐ understood and set my purpose for reading

As I read, I ...

- ☐ took notes
- ☐ looked for main ideas and tried to remember them
- ☐ stopped now and then to question myself
- ☐ looked for the answers to questions I had asked myself before I started reading
- ☐ stopped now and then to summarize the main ideas
- ☐ reread parts that I didn't understand
- ☐ used context clues to figure out words I didn't know

After I read, I

- ☐ thought about what I had learned
- ☐ summarized the main ideas

Put a **+** next to the strategy that you found the most helpful for understanding the selection. Explain why that strategy helped you.

_____

_____

_____

_____

Put a star next to the strategies that you didn't use but will use next time you read.

Activity – *Complete an evaluation form*

Reading-Study Strategy   reflect on thinking

Comprehension Focus   evaluate own strategic reading

Teaching Suggestions   After students complete the activity, conduct a **strategy conference** in which students share their reading-thinking strategies. During the discussion, encourage students to explain which strategies worked well for them, which strategies might have helped them more, and which strategies they used when their comprehension failed. Discuss the importance of evaluating one's strategic reading.

Previewing

Steps for Previewing

Previewing a selection is looking through it before you read to find out its content.

1 Read the chapter title.

2 Read the introductory paragraphs.

3 Decide the topic of the chapter. Ask yourself: *What is this chapter generally about?*

4 Identify important ideas and key words that relate to the topic.
• Read all the words and headings in bold print.
• If there are no bold headings, read the first sentence of each paragraph.

5 Look at pictures, charts, and diagrams and read their captions.

6 Read the conclusion, or summary paragraphs.

7 Read the questions at the end of the chapter. These may focus your attention on important ideas.

8 In your head, make a list of the important ideas that relate to the topic.

9 Think about what you already know about the topic and ideas.

10 Think about what you want to know about the topic and ideas.

Teaching Suggestions

Use the definition at the top of the *Strategy Guide* to define previewing. Explain to students that previewing improves comprehension because it focuses the reader's attention, enables the reader to recall background knowledge related to the general ideas, and helps the reader anticipate and predict the selection content.

Use the *Strategy Guide* to explain how to preview.

Model previewing.
- Make transparencies of pages of a textbook chapter.
- Project the pages onto a screen. Have students refer to the pages in their textbooks.
- Verbalize your mental processes as you preview the chapter. As you think aloud, use a marking pen or pointer to help students follow your thinking.

Skimming

> **Steps for Skimming a Selection**

> **Skimming** is reading quickly to find out what a selection is generally about. ◉◉

Read the title.

Read the first paragraph. Usually this paragraph gives the reader a good idea of what the selection is about.

Read all bold print headings.

Read the first sentence of each paragraph. ....

The first sentence often states the paragraph's main idea. ....

If you don't find a main idea statement, then move your eyes quickly down to the last sentence in the paragraph and read it. ....

Sometimes it states the main idea.

Read the heading.

As you move your eyes quickly over the lines in the paragraph, look for and read ....

.... **words in bold print** .... words in *italics* ....

.... names – Columbus .... dates – 1492

Keep reading quickly. ....

Read the last paragraph of the selection. Usually it gives a summary of the important ideas.

Strategy Guide – *Skimming*

Teaching Suggestions

Use the definition at the top of the *Strategy Guide* to define skimming. Explain that readers skim a selection before reading to get the gist, or main idea, of a selection. This knowledge helps the reader focus attention, anticipate content, and make predictions. Skimming is also a useful strategy to use after reading to review for tests or to locate information.

Use the *Strategy Guide* to show students how to skim. Point out that as they read the Guide, they are simulating skimming.

Model skimming.
- Make a transparency of a page from a reading selection all students have.
- Project the book page onto a screen. Have students refer to the page in their texts.
- Verbalize your mental processes as you skim the page. As you think aloud, move your finger along the transparency to show how your eyes move.

Students need to practice skimming. Provide opportunities for students to skim a selection and discuss what they learn. Ask different students to verbalize the process they use to skim.

Setting the Purpose for Reading

The **purpose for reading** is the goal or reason for reading a selection. Set your purpose for reading before you begin.

Steps for Setting the Purpose for Reading

Ask yourself these questions before you begin to read.

- What is my goal, or task?
- What will I be doing with the information in this selection?
- What do I want to get out of this reading selection?

Answer your questions.

There are several ways to find the answers to your questions.
- preview the selection and ask yourself questions
- preview the selection and decide what you hope to learn
- listen to what your teacher says
- listen to class discussions
- ask your teacher questions

Set your purpose.

Below are some different purposes you may set.
- read for enjoyment
- read to find the main ideas
- read to learn new information
- read to answer your own questions
- read to summarize important ideas

Now you are ready to choose the best reading strategy and begin reading. Remember to keep your purpose in mind as you read.

Teaching Suggestions

Use the definition at the top of the **Strategy Guide** to define purpose-setting. Explain to students that having a purpose, or goal, in mind improves comprehension because it focuses the reader's attention on key information. Also, knowing the purpose enables the reader to choose the best strategy for reading. For example, when the purpose is to read for enjoyment, a reader may choose to read at a normal, relaxed rate. However, if the purpose is to take a test, the reader may decide to read slowly and carefully and take notes.

Use the **Strategy Guide** to explain how to set a purpose for reading.

Model purpose-setting for students by verbalizing the mental processes you use to set your purposes for reading. Each time students read, ask them to identify their purposes.

Monitoring Comprehension

 During reading, good readers **monitor their comprehension**. They continually think about what they are reading and check to see whether they understand it. If they don't understand, they take action to correct the problem.

Steps for Monitoring Comprehension

 Think about the selection content as you read. Continually ask yourself:
Do I understand this?
Does this make sense?

 Stop reading at the end of a section or a page.
Say the important ideas to yourself.
Think about what you will be reading next.

 Continue reading

Sometimes you may not understand what you are reading and cannot say the important ideas to yourself. There are steps you can take to fix your failed understanding.

Steps for Fixing Failed Comprehension

 Reread the passages you don't understand.
Try again to say the important ideas to yourself.

If rereading does not correct the problem,

 Continue reading. See if your confusion is cleared up.
Then go back to the passage you didn't understand.
Try again to say the important ideas to yourself.

If reading ahead does not correct the problem,

 Ask for help.

Teaching Suggestions

Use the information at the top of the *Strategy Guide* to define comprehension monitoring. Explain to students that actively thinking about what they read and using fix-up strategies to help them when understanding fails will improve their comprehension and learning.

Use the *Strategy Guide* to explain to students how to monitor their comprehension and what to do when understanding fails.

Model comprehension monitoring.
- Make a transparency of a page from your textbook.
- Project the page onto a screen. Have students follow along in their books.
- Verbalize your mental processes as you read and monitor your comprehension. Be sure to model what you do when your understanding fails. As you think aloud, use a marking pen or pointer to help students follow along.

Understanding New Words

Four-Step Strategy for Understanding New Words

①  **Decide whether the word is important for understanding.**

The first thing to do when you come to a word you don't know is to finish reading the sentence or paragraph containing the word. Ask yourself:

Do I need to know the meaning of this word to understand what I am reading?

If yes,	If no,
go to step 2.	skip the word and continue reading.

②  **Look for context clues.**

Often you can figure out what a word means from the words and phrases around it. Read the sentences before and after the word. Look for words and phrases that give clues to the word's meaning.

If context clues don't help you figure out the word's meaning, go to step 3.	If there are good context clues and you now know what the word means, continue reading.

③ 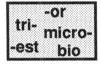 **Look for familiar word parts.**

You know the meanings of many word parts. Use their meanings to help you figure out what an unfamiliar word means. Sometimes you can use context clues along with word parts to define a word.

If you still cannot figure out the word's meaning, then go to step 4.	If you now know what the word means, continue reading.

④   **Look up the word in a dictionary or glossary.**

If you have followed all the steps and you still cannot figure out a word's meaning, look up the word.

Teaching Suggestions

Explain that when students come to an unfamiliar word as they read, they should not get frustrated and stop reading. Instead they should figure out the word's meaning.

Use the **Strategy Guide** to explain how to figure the meaning of an unfamiliar word.

Model the strategy.
- Make a transparency of paragraphs from the text.
- Project the paragraphs onto a screen. Have students refer to their books.
- Verbalize your mental processes as you use the four-step strategy to define unfamiliar words. As you think aloud, use a marking pen or a pointer to help students follow along.

Many students do not realize that it is permissible to skip a word that isn't key to understanding. In your modeling, provide examples to show instances of such words. Explain that you can go back to the word if you decide that it is important.

Using Context Clues

Context clues are other words and phrases in a sentence or paragraph that help you understand an unfamiliar word.

Steps for Using Context Clues

1 When you come to a word you do not know, finish reading the sentence or paragraph. Look for words and phrases that help you understand the word's meaning.

2 If there are no clues to help you define the word, reread the sentences that appear before the word. Look for context clues.

3 Reread the sentence containing the unfamiliar word and the context clues that you found. In your head, make up a definition for the word.

4 Check that your definition makes sense. Reread the sentence containing the word. Substitute your definition for the word. Does it make sense?
   If it does, then you have figured out the meaning of the word.
   If it doesn't, there may not be good context clues in the paragraph.

5 If there are no clues to help you figure out the word's meaning, look for familiar word parts or look up the word in a dictionary.

unfamiliar word

Lately, Jessica has been **dejected**. No one knows why she is so depressed and gloomy.

context clues

Teaching Suggestions

Use the definition at the top of the *Strategy Guide* and the example at the bottom of the page to define context clues.

Tell students that using context clues to define unknown words improves comprehension. Explain that when good readers come to words they don' t know, they don't stop reading. Instead they try to figure out the meaning of the new word by using context clues.

Use the *Strategy Guide* to explain how to use context clues.

Model using context clues.
- Make a transparency of paragraphs from the text.
- Project the paragraphs onto a screen. Have students refer to the paragraphs in their books.
- Verbalize your mental processes as you use context clues to define unfamiliar words. As you think aloud, use a marking pen or pointer to help students follow along.

Finding the Main Idea of a Paragraph

The **topic** of a paragraph is what the paragraph is mainly about. The topic is stated in one or two words.

The **main idea** of a paragraph is the most important idea about a topic. Often the main idea is stated in a sentence in the paragraph. Sometimes you must develop a sentence of your own to state the main idea.

Steps for Finding the Main Idea of a Paragraph

1 **Decide the topic of the paragraph.**

Ask yourself:

- *What is this paragraph mostly about?*
- *What one or two words state the topic?*

To find the topic:

- reread or skim the paragraph.
- read bold print headings.
- read words in bold print.
- look for a word or words that are repeated in several sentences.

2 **Find the main idea statement.**

Ask yourself:

- *What is the most important information about the topic?*

To find the main idea:

- reread the paragraph.
- look for a sentence that states the most important idea. Often it is the first or last sentence in the paragraph.

If the main idea is not stated in a sentence, go on to step 3.

3 **Develop your own main idea statement.**

Reread and think about all the examples and details that tell about the topic.
Think of one sentence that tells about the topic and all of the details.

- Begin your sentence with the word that states the paragraph topic.
- Complete your sentence with a statement that tells about all the details and examples.

Teaching Suggestions

Use the definitions at the top of the *Strategy Guide* to define topic and main idea. Explain that being able to identify main ideas will help students better understand, learn, and remember what they read. Remind students that finding main ideas is the first step in taking notes, writing summaries, and studying for tests.

Use the *Strategy Guide* to explain how to find main ideas of paragraphs.

Model finding the main idea.
- Make transparencies of paragraphs from the text. Choose examples with stated and unstated main ideas.
- Project the paragraphs onto a screen. Have students refer to the paragraphs in their books.
- Verbalize your mental processes as you decide a paragraph's topic and then either find a stated main idea or develop a main idea statement. As you think aloud, use different colored marking pens to underline main ideas and details.

Finding the Main Idea of a Selection

> The **topic** of a selection is what the selection is mainly about.
> The topic is stated in one or two words.
> The **main idea** of a selection is the most important idea about a topic.
> Often a writer discusses several main ideas that tell about the topic.

Steps for Finding the Main Idea of a Selection

■ Determine the selection topic.
  - Ask yourself: *What is this selection mostly about?* Say it in one or two words.
  - To find the topic, read the first paragraph and bold print headings.

■ Find the main idea or ideas.
A writer may develop one main idea or several main ideas that tell about the topic. Use the text organization to help you find the main ideas.

■ <u>Main Idea Organization 1</u>. The writer develops one main idea. Follow these steps.
  - Read the first paragraph. The main idea is usually stated.
  - Skim the rest of the selection to check that each paragraph tells about that main idea.
  - Read the last paragraph to see if the writer restates the main idea.

■ <u>Main Idea Organization 2</u>. The main ideas are stated in the first paragraph and restated in the last paragraph. Each idea is developed in the body of the selection. Follow these steps.
  - Read the first paragraph. Usually the main ideas are stated.
  - Skim the selection to check that each of those ideas is developed.
  - Read the last paragraph. Often the writer restates the main ideas.

■ <u>Main Idea Organization 3</u>. One main idea is developed in each section of a chapter. Follow these steps to find the main idea of each section.
  - Read the bold print heading and the first paragraph of the section. The main idea is usually stated.
  - Skim the section to check that the idea is developed.

■ <u>Main Idea Organization 4.</u> Each paragraph of the selection presents a new idea. To find the main ideas, read each paragraph and find its main idea.

Teaching Suggestions

Use the definitions at the top of the *Strategy Guide* to define topic and main idea. Explain that being able to identify main ideas will help students better understand, learn, and remember what they read. Remind students that finding main ideas is the first step in taking notes, writing summaries, and studying for tests.

Use the *Strategy Guide* to explain how to find main ideas of selections.

Model finding the main idea.
- Choose examples of each organizational pattern from classroom materials.
- Provide students with copies of the examples.
- Verbalize your mental processes as you decide a selection's topic and use the organizational pattern to find the main idea or ideas.

Have students work in *cooperative groups* to determine the main ideas of a variety of selections: magazine articles, textbook pages or chapters, essays, or newspaper editorials. Have a reporter from each group explain to the class how the group identified the main ideas.

Taking Notes

Steps for Taking Notes

1 Divide your paper into two columns.

> **Taking notes** is the process of selecting and organizing important information in a text.

2 In the left column, record

- key vocabulary words

- main ideas

3 In the right column, record

- definitions for vocabulary words

- details, examples, and facts that explain and illustrate the main ideas

 To find main ideas,

- Determine the topic of the paragraph or section. Say it in one or two words.
- Ask yourself: *What is the most important information about the topic?*
- Look for a sentence that states the most important idea.
  Often it is the first or last sentence in the paragraph.
- If the main idea is not stated, develop your own main idea statement.
  Write one sentence that tells about the topic and all of the details.

4 Use your notes as a study guide.
- Make questions from the information in one column.
- Cover up the information in the other column and test yourself.

Strategy Guide – *Taking Notes*

Teaching Suggestions

Explain to students that note-taking is a process of selecting and organizing important information. The key to good note-taking is recognizing main ideas and supporting details. Tell students that taking notes improves understanding and learning because it focuses the reader's attention on important ideas in the text. Notes also serve as a study guide for reviewing for a test.

Use the *Strategy Guide* to explain how to take notes.

Model taking notes.
- Make transparencies of a page from the text and a notebook page.
- Project the pages onto a screen. Have students follow along in their textbooks.
- First show students how you divide the paper into two columns. Then verbalize your mental processes as you take two-column notes from the textbook page. As you think aloud, use a marking pen or pointer to help students follow along.

To take notes successfully, students must understand how writers develop main ideas and how to select them. Use the *Finding Main Idea Strategy Guides*, pages 111 and 113, to teach and review finding main ideas. Use the *Is It Important?* activity on page 77 or the *Take Note!* activity on page 49 to provide practice with main ideas.

Students will need continual practice taking notes.
- Have students work in *cooperative groups* to take notes from a text and present them to the class.
- Regularly assign note-taking for homework. Have students take notes from one section of their textbooks at a time.

Writing a Summary

 Steps for Writing a Summary

A **summary** retells the most important ideas in a selection.

1 **Make a chart like the one below.**

TOPIC _____	
main ideas	*important details*

2 **Fill in the chart with information from the selection.**

- <u>Topic</u>   Write one or two words that tell what the selection is mainly about.
- <u>Main Ideas</u>   List the most important ideas that tell about the topic.
- <u>Important Details</u>   List important details that go with a main idea.
  Limit the number of details you include. You may find there are none.

3 **Reread and check the information in your chart.**

- Add important ideas you left out.
- Cross out information that is not important.
- Cross out information that repeats.

4 **Write sentences using the information in the chart.**

- Write a sentence that states the topic.
- Write a sentence that states each main idea.
  Include important details that go with that idea.
- Put your sentences in the correct order.

5 **Write your summary. Use your sentences.**

- Use words and phrases such as "first," "next," "in addition," "explains that,"
  "presents," and "discusses."
- Combine sentences.

6 **Revise and edit your summary. Then copy it onto a clean sheet of paper.**

- Check that you included only the important information.
- Check that you left out nothing important.
- Read your summary aloud to check that it reads smoothly and makes sense.
- Cross out unnecessary words.
- Check that words are spelled correctly.

Strategy Guide – *Summarizing*

Teaching Suggestions

Use the definition at the top of the *Strategy Guide* to define summary. Tell students that writing summaries helps them learn and remember important information.

Use the *Strategy Guide* to explain how to write a summary. Tell students that as they follow the steps to write their summaries, they will need to skim and reread parts of the material several times in order to select main ideas and check back with the text often to ensure that they get the most important ideas.

> Before students can be good summarizers, they must be able to distinguish main ideas from details. Use the *Main Idea Strategy Guides* on pages 111 and 113 to review main idea.

Model writing a summary.
- Make a transparency of a short, well-written selection. Provide students with a copy.
- Project the selection onto a screen.
- Verbalize your mental processes as you summarize the selection. As you think aloud, use a marking pen or pointer to help students follow along.

Students need continual practice writing summaries.
- As a regular homework assignment, have students write a summary paragraph for a section of a chapter of their textbooks.
- Have students work in *cooperative groups* to write summaries of the same selection and present them.

ALSO AVAILABLE FROM SPRING STREET PRESS ...

Responding to Literature
Grades 1-3

- 58 creative Response Activities
- 8 Record-Keeping Charts
- teaching ideas for ESL students
- suggestions for developing oral language skills

..............................$15.95

Responding to Literature: Writing and Thinking Activities

- contains generic activities that go with <u>any</u> selection
- integrates reading and writing
- promotes creative and critical thinking
- extends reading beyond the selection

Each book is packed with fully reproducible reading Response Activities that can be used with any reading selection and Record-Keeping Charts to assist you in monitoring and managing students' reading. The Response Activities may be used in a variety of ways to adapt to your reading curriculum and teaching style as well as to the varied abilities and learning styles of your students.

Typical response activities include writing in all forms – narrative, descriptive persuasive and expository – and in a variety of modes – poems, letters, short stories, news stories, journal entries and many, many more. Motivating and imaginative activities such as creating advertisements, book jackets, coats of arms, and tee shirt slogans capture students' attention and hold their interest.

Responding to Literature
Grades 4-8

- 75 open-ended Response Activities
- 8 Record-Keeping Charts

..............................$15.95

AVAILABLE IN SPANISH
Motivando La Lectura
Actividades de Razonamiento en Torno a la Literatura

Motivando la Lectura
Grados 1-3
..........................$16.95

Motivando la Lectura
Grados 4-8
..........................$16.95

HELP STUDENTS BECOME STRATEGIC READERS AND LEARNERS

Strategies for Reading Nonfiction
Comprehension and Study Activities
Grades 4-8

- contains over 40 reproducible Comprehension and Study Activities plus 10 Strategy Guides
- may be used with any nonfiction selection
    - textbooks
    - trade books
    - articles and essays
- provides a variety of activities that help students read, understand and learn from expository text

..............................$15.95

Prereading and follow-up postreading activities develop strategic readers.

Guided reading strategies help students monitor their comprehension and think as they read.

Study and writing activities help students read for main ideas, summarize, and write expository paragraphs.

Strategy Guides help students apply key reading-study skills including setting purpose for reading, previewing and predicting, and taking notes.

ORDER FORM

Name _____

Shipping Address _____

_____

City _____ State _____ Zip _____

Qty.	Title	Price	Amt.
	Responding to Literature gr. 1-3	$15.95	$
	Responding to Literature gr. 4-8	$15.95	$
	Strategies / Nonfiction gr. 4-8	$15.95	$
	Motivando La Lectura gr. 1-3	$16.95	$
	Motivando La Lectura gr. 4-8	$16.95	$
	Shipping & Handling (see chart for amt.)		$
	TOTAL ENCLOSED (All payments must be in US Funds.)		$

Shipping Charges		in US	to Canada
1	book	4.00	4.50
2	books	4.50	5.00
3-5	books	5.50	6.00
6-9	books	7.25	11.00
10-15	books	11.00	14.00

**Mail orders with payment to
Spring Street Press
2606 Spring Blvd.
Eugene, OR 97403**

Payment Method:

☐ Check   ☐ VISA/Mastercard

Credit Card Number_____ Expiration Date _____

Signature _____

(Credit card charges must have signature.)